CONTENTS

WELCOME TO
OXFORD BOTANIC GARDEN

OXFORD BOTANIC GARDEN is the United Kingdom's oldest botanic garden. It was founded as the Oxford Physicke Garden in 1621 by Henry Danvers, 1st Earl of Danby KG, for the cultivation of medicinal plants for the University of Oxford's medical students. The Garden therefore occupies a unique place in history and academic location as the birthplace of botanical science in the UK.

Today Oxford Botanic Garden remains a centre for plant science research and teaching. Its mission is 'to share the scientific wonder and importance of plants with the world'. Together with its sister site, the Harcourt Arboretum, it holds a collection of over 5,000 different types of plant. Some are extremely rare in the wild and some exist nowhere else in the world, making the collection internationally important for plant conservation.

This guide will enable you to get more from your visit to the Oxford Botanic Garden, to learn why we grow the plants we do, what they are used for and why plants are critical for all life on earth.

THE HISTORIC WALLED GARDEN

The Walled Garden is the oldest part of the Garden and was the original Physicke Garden. It was built between 1621 and 1639 and planted in the 1640s by the first keeper, Jacob Bobart the Elder. Today it houses the Taxonomic Beds (which demonstrate the genetic and evolutionary relatedness of the flowering plants), the Wall Borders (a group of geographic and historic plant collections), the Medicinal Plant Beds, the Literary Woodland and the Herbarium Room.

Discover more about the diversity and evolution of flowering plants in the historic Walled Garden against the backdrop of the seventeenth-century walls and the monumental Danby Gate.

THE HISTORIC WALLS AND DANBY GATE

Physic gardens (originally 'physicke' or 'physick') are collections of medicinal plants used in the teaching of herbal medicine. The oldest physic garden is at Padua, Italy, and was founded in 1533. During the second half of the sixteenth century physic gardens became established at major university cities in Italy (Pisa, 1544, Florence, 1545, and Bologna, 1568) and across Europe (Leiden, 1577, Montpellier, 1593, Heidelberg, 1593, and Paris, 1597). Their plant collections helped medical students and teachers to recognize the plants required for their herbal medicines; indeed, mistakenly prescribing the wrong plants could be fatal!

Henry Danvers recognized the need for a physic garden in England, and, as Stephen Harris notes in his book *Oxford Botanic Garden & Arboretum: A Brief History* (Bodleian Library, 2017), 'being minded to become a benefactor to the University [of Oxford]', gave the sum of £250 to buy the lease to 2 hectares of low-lying pasture beside the River Cherwell. This land, owned by Magdalen College, was leased by the university for 40 shillings a year. Between 1621 and 1636, the land was raised above the river with 4,000 loads of 'mucke and dunge' and stonemasons enclosed it with a wall 4.3 metres high and over 500 metres in length. Together with the four gates the total cost to Danvers exceeded £5,000.

The grand north entrance gate (the 'Danby Gate') is one of the iconic structures of Oxford Botanic Garden and indeed Oxford. A glimpse through this gate into the historic Walled Garden is among the city's classic views. The gate, originally with a large wood-panelled door, was designed by Inigo Jones and built by Charles I's master mason, Neklaus Stone, at a cost of £500 (over £60,000 today), and was completed in 1632. The features in the ornate, stone arch include the arms of Henry Danvers, the university, St George and the House of Stuart. The figures of Charles I and Charles II were added by the university in 1693. Above the main entrance in a segmented niche is a bust of Danvers. Of the other three major gates, the smaller East Gate (towards the River Cherwell) and the West Gate (towards Rose Lane) are both original and similar in design to the Danby Gate. Today's South Gate, at the entrance to the Lower Garden, is very different and largely an amalgam of eighteenth-century and more recent architecture. Additional small gates were also inserted into the south and north walls in the eighteenth century and one of these is now the public entrance to the Garden.

One of the small gates inserted into the south wall of the Walled Garden in the eighteenth century.

Illustration by Augustus Welby Pugin showing the Botanic Garden's Danby Gate in 1816.

OPPOSITE The magnificent historic Danby Gate, viewed from within the Walled Garden.

THE WALL BORDERS

A wild-collected flowering specimen of *Kirengeshoma palmata*.

Plants in the Wall Borders include the Garden's geographic collections from Japan, Chile and New Zealand. These three countries are biodiversity hotspots of exceptional species richness and conservation importance, while New Zealand also represents a unique isolated island flora (like the Galapagos Islands) of great significance in understanding the processes of evolution. Around the world there are thirty-five biodiversity hotspots, which cover just 2.3 per cent of the earth's land surface, but they support more than half of the world's endemic plant species.

Of particular importance are the Japanese plants in the south-west border, which have been raised from seed collected by staff as part of a major collaborative research and conservation project with the Botanic Gardens of Toyama in Japan, Oxford's Department of Plant Sciences and Kew's Millennium Seed Bank.

Japan is a narrow island archipelago with a wide range of climates, from the subarctic region of Hokkaido in the north to subtropical island of Okinawa in the south, and is home to more than 7,000 plant species. The country's flora covers three different ecozones (major biogeographic divisions), namely Palearctic, Indomalayan and Oceanian. The islands are surrounded by ocean on all sides and have a varied and complex inland geography. This has contributed to the exceptional diversity of the Japanese flora. Oxford Botanic Garden's 'Japan Project' has been carried out for a period of over

six years with partners in Japan and the UK to conserve this exceptionally diverse flora. During this time, seed from nearly 400 different plant species has been collected, and thousands of herbarium voucher specimens have been made.

Virtually all of the familiar plants in this border, such as the *Hosta*, were collected from natural populations in Japan. Other plants of interest here include the white-flowered *Aster glenhii* var. *hondensis* and rare yellow toad lilies (*Tricyrtis latifolia*), ferns (*Drypoteris cycadina*) and unusual shrubs like *Kirengeshoma palmata*. Important tree species in this conservation collection are cultivated at the Harcourt Arboretum, for instance the critically endangered birch, *Betula chichibuensis*, of which there are few trees remaining in the wild.

OPPOSITE Plants in this bed, such as the *Hosta* in the foreground, were raised from seed collected by staff of the Botanic Garden and Harcourt Arboretum in Japan.

THE TAXONOMIC BEDS

When the Garden was first established as a physic garden in 1621, many of the plants were classified according to their medicinal properties. Later, in the mid-1800s, they were rearranged by geographical origin as more specimens became available from abroad. Today the Taxonomic Beds showcase evolution, diversity and classification in flowering plants, and are a living library for teaching and research in plant evolutionary biology. These beds house thousands of different plants and make up much of the Walled Garden.

The evolution of plants has long fascinated scientists, not least Charles Darwin, who described the origin and early evolution of flowering plants as 'an abominable mystery'. Our most modern and objective means of classifying flowering plants is known as the Angiosperm Phylogeny Group (APG) system. Unlike former classifications based on plants' morphology (their appearance), APG uses DNA sequence data, and is therefore reflective of their genetic and evolutionary relatedness. For example, today we recognize that the basal angiosperms contain the most ancient surviving lineages of flowering plants, the now-extinct ancestors of which existed over 120 million years ago at the time of the last dinosaurs. This assemblage of plants is unusual in its diverse flower forms and is more closely related to the magnoliids (such as magnolias and laurels) and monocots (lilies and irises, for instance) than to the rest of the flowering plants, collectively called the eudicots. The latest version of APG (APG IV) includes 416 families and many thousands of species.

All the plants in the Taxonomic Beds have been reorganized into groups to follow APG IV. This process took four years and was completed in 2019.

The recently reconfigured Taxonomic Beds.

THE MEDICINAL PLANT BEDS

The south-west corner of the Botanic Garden is home to the medicinal plant collection. This collection features plants that were grown when the Garden was established in the 1600s as a physic garden. Indeed, a catalogue produced by the Garden's first keeper in 1648 gives precise information about which species were cultivated. Today the beds show how plants have been used in medicine traditionally, and how they are now important in modern clinical medicine. Plants are cultivated in eight beds, each containing species with connections to medicines for treating various types of disease or illness, including: cardiology (heart complaints); oncology (cancer and cell proliferation); dermatology (skin complaints); gastroenterology (alimentary tract); pulmonology (lungs and airways), and many more.

The plants growing in these beds contain many different natural products, and are either directly suitable as a drug, synthetically modifiable to provide a clinically suitable drug or represent the starting point for a drug-discovery programme. Some are very familiar, such as the foxglove genus (*Digitalis*) from which the drug digoxin, a remedy for heart arrhythmias, is isolated. Other plants supply us with a key intermediate that is transformed into a chemical employed in treatment. For example, etoposide, which is used to treat certain cancers, is a semi-synthetic derivative of a substance extracted from *Podophyllum hexandrum*.

Screaming mandrakes

Mandrakes (*Mandragora officinarum*) have been grown at Oxford Botanic Garden since 1648 and used in herbal medicine since antiquity. They belong to the same family as potatoes and tomatoes (Solanaceae) and are native to the Mediterranean Basin. The root of the mandrake is long, fleshy and contorted, and sometimes vaguely resembles a human figure. For this reason, and because of its potent properties, the plant is shrouded by myth, and has a very rich folklore and history of medicinal use. For example, the mandrake was once

Mandrakes (*Mandragora officinarum*) have been grown at Oxford Botanic Garden since at least 1648.

Deadly nightshade

Deadly nightshade (*Atropa belladonna*) and its relatives henbane (*Hyoscyamus niger*) and thorn-apple (*Datura stramonium*) can all be seen in the Medicinal Plant Beds, in varying abundance from year to year, depending on the weather. These plants belong to the same family as the mandrake and are very poisonous in large quantities. Deadly nightshade has a long history as a medicine, cosmetic and poison. The name *'belladonna'* is derived from 'bellum' (commemorating Bellona, the goddess of war) and 'donum' (the gift of war) in reference to the plant's deadly properties. Eye drops containing the herb were used by women to dilate the pupils of their eyes to make them appear seductive.

Birthwort

Although now known to be poisonous, birthwort (*Aristolochia clematitis*) was used as a medicinal plant centuries ago, and is still occasionally found established outside of its native range as a relic of cultivation. The plant was administered to ease childbirth, probably due to the unusual uterus-like shape of its flowers. The belief that the resemblance of a plant to a part of the human body indicates its ability to cure/treat ailments to that body part is known as the doctrine of signatures and has existed since the time of Dioscorides (1st century CE) and Galen (2nd–3rd century CE). Another example is the lungwort (*Pulmonaria officinalis*), once employed to treat pulmonary infections because its spotted lung-shaped leaves were thought to 'signature' diseased, ulcerated lungs.

Deadly nightshade (*Atropa belladonna*).

believed to be an aphrodisiac. The plant has hallucinogenic properties and was also widely employed as an anaesthetic.

In the *Harry Potter* books a mandrake lets out a fatal shriek when uprooted. Indeed, historically the mandrake was believed to shriek and to kill whoever uprooted it. To uproot a mandrake safely, it was thought that it must be tethered to a dog.

The plant can be seen in flower in February and March and produces berry-like fruits in early summer.

ABOVE AND TOP LEFT Ornamental opium poppies (*Papaver somniferum*) are a source of opiate drugs which are extracted from opium.

LEFT *Aristolochia rotunda*, a relative of the birthwort (*Aristolochia clematitis*).

THE LITERARY WOODLAND

The Garden's trees are, of course, the longest-standing living features of the ever-changing design and landscape. The white mulberry (*Morus alba*), hornbeam (*Carpinus betulus*) and buckthorn (*Rhamnus cathartica*) are the sole survivors of four geographically focused tree collections that were planted in the 1800s. Three other trees exceeding 150 years in age are the service tree (*Sorbus domestica*) (planted 1795) and whitty pear (*Sorbus domestica*) (planted 1850) in the Walled Garden, and the black walnut (*Juglans nigra*) (planted 1860) in the Lower Garden. The oldest of the Garden's majestic trees, however, is an

The Literary Woodland.

English yew (*Taxus baccata*) planted in 1645 by the Garden's first keeper, Jacob Bobart the Elder. The sole remaining tree is one of many yews that were planted, most of which were removed by Charles Daubeny, the Sherardian Professor of Botany, in the 1800s.

The collection of trees and large shrubs that grows at the southern end of the Walled Garden today provides shade and the feel of a woodland. In February 2017 work began to develop this woodland area by extending the existing black mulberry (*Morus nigra*) bed and English yew bed to create a 'Literary Woodland' to showcase plants that appear in English literature, and especially in Oxford's rich literary heritage. Here you will find a smiling Cheshire Cat in the black mulberry tree above some of the 'talking flowers' (notably tiger lilies, larkspur and daisies) that feature in *Alice's Adventures in Wonderland* and *Through the Looking Glass*. Charles Dodgson (Lewis Carroll) and Alice Liddell were regular visitors to the Botanic Garden. This literary theme also connects with the Lower Garden where you can find 'Lyra and Will's bench' set among plants of the arctic Svalbard, recalling Philip Pullman's trilogy *His Dark Materials* (1995–2000).

Cheshire Cat in the black mulberry tree (sculpture by Julian Warren, better known as 'Metalgnu').

THE HERBARIUM ROOM

The Herbarium Room is the Garden's 'mini museum', designed to display botanical treasures from the Oxford University Herbaria, one of the most important collections of dried plants and other botanical objects in the world. Today the Herbaria is housed in the university's Department of Plant Sciences (Botany) and is open to the public during special exhibitions. The Herbarium Room reconnects the Garden with the Herbaria, which up until the 1950s was located in the buildings adjoining it, which formed the Department of Botany.

The design of the room is inspired by Swedish botanist Carl Linnaeus's residence in Hammarby, Sweden, and its famous wallpaper created by the great botanical artist Georg Dionysius Ehret. The walls of the room are decorated with facsimiles of botanical drawings from the *Hortus Elthamensis* published in 1732, which is housed in the Herbaria. This 'botanical treasure' was written and illustrated by Johann Jacob Dillenius, Oxford's first Sherardian Professor of Botany, and documents exotic plants cultivated by wealthy, early eighteenth-century apothecary James Sherard at Eltham in Kent. Two hundred and forty of the 325 plates of the *Hortus* form the Herbarium Room's unique 'wallpaper'. The room's curtains take their design from the drawing of the night-flowering *Hylocereus* cactus, which can be seen growing in the Arid House (see page 48–51).

In the display cabinets you will find a changing series of themed exhibitions featuring pressed plants and other botanical objects from the Oxford University Herbaria. These specimens are important scientific records and provide evidence of which species were growing at a particular point in time and place. They were originally amassed here at the Botanic Garden when it housed the Department of Botany. The Herbaria contains material from four centuries of global exploration, including some of the first specimens collected in North America, China, Brazil and Africa. Living examples of these unique plant discoveries can be seen growing in the Garden today as testimony to this rich botanical history.

The Herbarium Room, the design of which is inspired by the Swedish botanist Carl Linneaus's residence at Hammarby in Sweden, reconnects the garden with the Oxford Herbaria. The walls feature plates from the *Hortus Elthamensis* and the cabinets contain important specimens from the Herbaria.

THE GLASSHOUSES

The glasshouses offer a range of climatic conditions in which we grow plants from warmer parts of the world. Here you can visit tropical jungles and cloud forests or an arid desert in the space of just a few metres. The first glasshouse was built at the Botanic Garden more than 300 years ago. It was a temperate conservatory, which resembled an orangery and was used to house tender and exotic plants, such as cacti, succulents and citrus, during the cold winter months.

THE HISTORY OF GLASSHOUSE CULTIVATION AT THE GARDEN

In 1834 Professor Charles Daubeny embarked on a scientific mission of transformation at the Garden. He commissioned the building of a stove house (a heated greenhouse) in 1835 in which his able curator William Baxter grew palms, bananas and orchids. But after seeing the giant Amazonian water lily (*Victoria amazonica*) flowering for the first time in Britain at Chatsworth House, Daubeny's ambitions expanded, and in 1851 he and Baxter constructed two ranges of glasshouses either side of the East Gate, one containing a pool (still there to this day) in which to grow the giant water lily. In 1853 *Victoria amazonica* flowered at Oxford and was a sensation in the city, despite Daubeny charging people a shilling to see it.

The present layout of the glasshouses dates to the 1800s, but the aluminium superstructures were built in 1971.

The central raised pool in the Water Lily House was built in 1851 for the cultivation of the giant Amazonian water lily (*Victoria amazonica*), which can be seen in the background. The leaves at the very back with higher edges belong to *V. cruziana*, a close relative which is cultivated in the Water Lily House annually. The floating aquatic plant in the foreground is the water lettuce (*Pistia stratiotes*).

THE CONSERVATORY

Citrus plants, including lemons, limes, oranges, mandarins, grapefruits and citrons, have been grown at the Botanic Garden since the 1600s. From late spring, the fragrant scent of their flowers fills the Conservatory. When conditions are right, the plants flower and bear fruit simultaneously throughout much of the year. Citrus is not only used to make fruit juice. Eau de cologne, Cointreau, Earl Grey tea, marmalade and suntan oil are just some of the many products containing this economically important genus. Indeed, citrus cultivation is the most important fruit industry in warm parts of the world such as Australia, California, South Africa and the Mediterranean Basin. In Asia citrus fruits have also been an ingredient in local and commercial medicinal preparations for centuries.

The evolutionary origins of the different species of citrus are complex as most are

hybrids. *Citrus medica*, growing here, is a particularly large-fruited species and was the first to be introduced to Europeans. Alexander the Great brought it to the Mediterranean and later it featured prominently in Roman life, as recorded in frescoes at Pompeii. In the eighth century an intriguing form of *C. medica*, with fruits possessing finger-like projections, was introduced to China where it is still used to scent rooms and to flavour tea. Called *Citrus medica* var. *sarcodactylis*, it is sold by florists in the Mediterranean today as a curiosity, where it is often fancifully called the 'Buddha's hand'. Our specimen is usually weighed down with several spectacular fruits and is a popular feature of the Conservatory.

Other notable plants in the Conservatory include the large Madeira cranesbill (*Geranium maderense*), the seasonal displays of orchids, scented pelargoniums and winter bulbs (narcissi and hyacinths).

OPPOSITE The Conservatory houses a wide variety of plants from around the world including cycads, palms and citrus, and assorted exotic house plants. Seasonal displays feature potted orchids, scented pelargoniums and winter bulbs.

ABOVE RIGHT The 'Buddha's hand' (*Citrus medica* var. *sarcodactylis*).

BELOW RIGHT Potted auriculas (*Primula auricula*), an example of a plant cultivated by the Garden's first keeper, Bobart the Elder, in the seventeenth century.

PLANTS FROM HIGH PLACES

The plants cultivated in this small temperate house originate from across the globe. The plants are pot-grown and sunk into the raised beds in a seasonal rotation, so there is always something different for visitors to enjoy. Many of the plants are alpines and grow well in the cool British winter under glass.

In spring orchids such as the peculiar tongue orchid (*Serapias lingua*), native to the

Dead horse arum (*Helicodiceros muscivorus*).

Mediterranean, can be seen in flower here. In nature, solitary bees rest inside the tunnel of the tongue orchids' flowers, and remain there overnight or during wet weather. The bees that visit the tongue orchids typically seek refuge in holes in the ground and it is hypothesized that the tongue orchids have evolved to mimic these protective shelters in order to attract insect pollinators. Another curiosity of this house is the spectacular dead horse arum (*Helicodiceros muscivorus*), which blooms in March. This strange plant is native to the clifftops of the central Mediterranean islands

The peculiar tongue orchid (*Serapias lingua*).

and its floral structures resemble the corpse of a dead animal, both in appearance and smell. These noxious features attract flies, which swarm around it, looking for a place to lay their eggs. Soon fooled, they crawl into a waxy chamber in which they lose their footing and become trapped. By the time the flies escape, they are covered in pollen, which they unwittingly transport to the next dead horse arum they encounter, thereby promoting cross-pollination.

More conventionally attractive plants cultivated in these display beds include beautiful stands of *Narcissus* daffodils in late winter, and a range of bulbs and perennials throughout the summer months, such as so-called pineapple lilies (*Eucomis*), alliums and various orchid species.

Potted cyclamens (*Cyclamen graecum*).

THE WATER LILY HOUSE

The Water Lily House offers a glimpse into tropical Amazonia. Its central raised pool dates from 1851, when it was built for the cultivation of the giant Amazonian water lily (*V. amazonica*). We now normally grow the more manageable species, *Victoria cruziana*, which is very similar. The giant Amazonian water lily is native to the shallow waters of the Amazon basin. It is the largest of the water lilies, and its gigantic leaves can span almost 3 metres across. Also growing in the pond is the beautiful day-blooming *Nymphaea x daubenyana*, which produces scented, long-lasting lilac flowers. This hybrid water lily was first propagated here in 1874. It was named in honour of Professor Daubeny, the Sherardian Professor and keeper of the Garden from 1834 to 1867.

All the plants growing in the pool are adapted to an aquatic existence. For example, the water lilies have hollow stems that keep their leaves and flowers afloat, and the leaves of the sacred lotus (*Nelumbo nucifera*) have water-repellent surfaces, while the mangroves have specialized roots with 'breathing holes' that grow vertically above the surface of the water and mud. At the margins of the pond is the plant that feeds more people on the planet than any other food: rice (*Oryza sativa*). There are as many as 120,000 varieties of cultivated rice, providing an annual global harvest in excess of 520 million tonnes. Bananas (*Musa*) can also be seen in the jungle-like borders surrounding the pool.

ABOVE The hybrid water lily *Nymphaea x daubenyana* which was first propagated at Oxford Botanic Garden in 1874.

OPPOSITE The Water Lily House is home to a rich assortment of tropical aquatics such as the Amazonian water lily (*Victoria amazonica*), as well as banana plants (*Musa*), potted bromeliads and orchids, and *Nepenthes* pitcher plants in suspended baskets.

THE CLOUD FOREST HOUSE

The inspiration for this small house is the tropical plant paradise of Mount Kinabalu in the north of Borneo. At 4,095 metres, this is the highest mountain in the Malay Archipelago and is a World Heritage Site famous for its numerous endemic orchids and carnivorous *Nepenthes* pitcher plants. The latter form an important resource for research carried out by scientists at the Garden and in the Department of Plant Sciences into the biology and evolution of this fascinating genus.

The leafy traps of *Nepenthes* pitcher plants evolved where soils are poor to derive nutrients from insects. Insects are attracted to their nectar and fall from the slippery rim into a

ABOVE A carnivorous pitcher plant (*Nepenthes sanguinea*).

RIGHT The world's largest pitcher plant, *Nepenthes rajah*, photographed here on its native Mount Kinabalu in Borneo.

The Cloud Forest House is dripping with ferns, orchids and carnivorous pitcher plants, the latter of which are an area of research focus at the garden.

pool of digestive juices. The pitchers have a vast assortment of shapes and sizes and are adapted to extracting nutrients from a number of sources: from insects to leaf litter, and even sometimes animal faeces. Our research at the Garden indicates that this variation in diet has probably played an important role in the evolution of pitcher form among species.

THE CARNIVOROUS PLANT HOUSE

All carnivorous plants evolved in environments where nutrients are scarce, such as water-logged swamps or rain-leached mountain slopes. These 'green predators' produce an array of lures and traps to attract, catch and digest animal prey to supplement their diet. There are nearly 600 species and it is now known that they evolved several times independently. Their traps range from simple structures, such as tightly bound leaf rosettes that retain water, to intricate forms with unique strategies for capturing and killing specific types of prey.

Darwin was fascinated by carnivorous plants. He studied their feeding mechanisms carefully, offering them meat and glass, blowing on them and prodding them with hair. He concluded that the movement of an animal caused the plants to react.

One of the most popular specimens in the Carnivorous Plant House is the Venus flytrap (*Dionaea muscipula*). This carnivore inhabits

the subtropical wetlands of North and South Carolina. The leafy jaws comprise a barbed snare that is triggered by prey brushing against the minute hairs on the inner surface. The lobes compress together tightly, forming a sealed cavity within which the soft parts of the insects are digested. Other plants in this house include trumpet pitchers (*Sarracenia*), which have pitfall traps containing pools of digestive juices into which insects tumble, and sundews (*Drosera*), which ensnare insect prey with a sticky, glue-like substance on the surface of their leaves.

The plants in this house lie dormant in the winter months, and are best seen from May to September.

Venus flytraps (*Dionaea muscipula*).
Trumpet pitchers (*Sarracenia leucophylla*).
Trumpet pitchers (*Sarracenia flava*).

(left) The pitchers of a *Sarracenia* hybrid in the Carnivorous Plant House.
(right) An assortment of pitcher plants (*Heliamphora* and *Sarracenia*) are grown in the Carnivorous Plant House.

THE RAINFOREST HOUSE

This is the largest of the individual houses and gives the visitor a tropical rainforest experience. Palms, an ancient lineage of plants, are an important component of the understorey of most tropical rainforests, and many can be seen growing in the Rainforest House. The palm family (Arecaceae) contains about 2,600 species, most of which are native to the tropics. Many are an edible delicacy for animals, including humans; one yields a prized ingredient ('palm hearts') used in Far Eastern cooking. Palms are also the source of palm oil, the demand and production of which has led to the destruction of vast areas of tropical rainforest worldwide.

Competition among plants in rainforests is fierce, as they jostle for light and space. With no cold season to halt their growth, and

ABOVE The tiny flowers of cocoa (*Theobroma cacao*).
OPPOSITE AND OVERLEAF The Rainforest House.

a plentiful supply of water, rainforest plants can grow at a phenomenal rate. Some, such as the *Alocasia*, have enormous leaves, making the most of available light as it filters down through the canopy. Meanwhile, climbers and rattans (climbing palms) compete with other plants in their search for light, while epiphytes (plants, like orchids and bromeliads, that grow on other plants) perch high up in the canopy. An inconspicuous but curious plant that can be seen growing in the Palm House is *Dorstenia*, which produces peculiar, green fruiting structures. Research carried out by our scientists suggests that this plant may offer insights into the evolution of the fig, to which it is related.

We also grow several economically important plants in the Palm House, which are a valuable education resource. Vines of black pepper (*Piper nigrum*) – the most widely traded spice – can be seen, along with cocoa trees (*Theobroma cacao*) – the source of cocoa beans (and chocolate) – on the left of the glasshouse. Cotton (*Gossypium arboreum*), complete with its hairy fruits, features in the central beds. Other useful plants include rubber (*Ficus elastica*), pineapples (*Ananas comosus*) and small stands of sugar cane (*Saccharum officinarum*).

The Rainforest House is a year-round attraction for visitors to the Garden.

The peculiar fruiting structure of *Dorstenia,* a relative of the fig.

The fruiting head of a cotton (*Gossypium arboreum*).

THE ARID HOUSE

All the plants in this house are adapted to extreme drought. In nature, many of these plants take up water rapidly and store it in their succulent stems and leaves during infrequent periods of rainfall. Some of these plants feature 'crassulacean acid metabolism' (CAM), a particularly efficient adaptation for photosynthesis in which their pores (stomata) remain closed during the day to reduce water loss. At night these pores then open to absorb carbon dioxide, which is stored as malic acid until required for photosynthesis in daylight.

Rainfall usually triggers flowering in arid plant communities and mass flowerings often coincide with the migration of pollinating birds. Other species flower at dusk when pollinating bats emerge, for example cacti such as the dragon fruit (*Hylocereus undatus*), which produces enormous, and very beautiful, cream flowers that wither by sunrise. In August and September, the shrivelled giant, cabbage-sized cream flowers can be seen littering the floor of the Arid House: they last for just a single night.

Among the most prominent specimens in the Arid House are the giant euphorbia (*Euphorbia abyssinica*) and, next to it, a cactus (*Cereus uruguayanus*), which stand over 6 metres tall in the centre and are believed to be nearly two centuries old. These plants evolved on the continents of Africa and South America respectively. Because they both evolved adaptations to survive arid conditions, they look very similar, even though they belong to unrelated families, Euphorbiaceae and Cactaceae: a classic example of convergent evolution. The Old World aloes (Asphodelaceae) and New World agaves (Asparagaceae) in this house represent a further example of convergent evolution and collectively serve as a valuable teaching resource at all levels.

Some aloe and agave species are also of commercial or local importance. *Aloe vera*, for example, is a succulent, the sap from which is

The spectacular flower of the dragon fruit cactus (*Hylocereus undatus*).

found in many consumer products, including cosmetics, sunscreens, shampoos and 'after-sun' ointments. Agaves, such as *Agave tequilana*, are used in tequila production and to make a sugar substitute ('agave nectar'). Agaves were often referred to as 'century plants' because it was believed that they took a century or more to flower. In fact, under warm conditions, they may take far less time than this. Interestingly, each giant rosette is monocarpic, meaning it flowers only once and then dies.

THE LOWER GARDEN

The Lower Garden holds ornamental collections, including the Rock Garden, which has many Mediterranean species, the magnificent Herbaceous Border, the Merton Borders, the Plants that Changed the World Borders, the Gin Border, in which gin 'botanicals' are grown, and the Water Garden. With the River Cherwell and Christ Church Meadow as its boundaries, the Lower Garden provides a tranquil space, perfect for picnics and relaxation.

The main body of the Lower Garden, below the lily pond, is a relatively recent addition to Oxford Botanic Garden. Originally part of Christ Church Meadow, this 1.2-hectare portion was leased from Christ Church in 1944. During the Second World War the area was used to grow vegetables as part of the 'Dig for victory' campaign and in 1947 these 'allotments' became fully incorporated into the Botanic Garden.

THE ROCK GARDEN

The Rock Garden was first constructed in 1926 and since then has been reconfigured roughly once every twenty-five years. The most recent redesign took place between 1997 and 1999 when 125 tonnes of sandstone were brought to the Garden from a local quarry in Tubney, about 10 kilometres west of Oxford.

The plants on the east side are mainly European in origin, while many of those on the west side are from other parts of the world. These beds enable us to cultivate plants that require specific conditions not achievable elsewhere in the Garden. In late winter there is a fine display of snowdrops, followed by species tulips in the spring. A number of *Euphorbia* species also prosper here, such as the Mediterranean species: *E. rigida*, *E. myrsinites* and *E. spinosa*. In the summer months other perennials come into bloom, including the pink-flowered *Acanthus dioscoridis* and the graceful, arching stems of *Dierama pulcherrimum*.

The Rock Garden is currently entering a new phase of redesign and reconfiguration to show plants from Greece and the Levant that were first collected by the Sherardian Professor of Botany, John Sibthorp. His two expeditions of 1786–7 and 1794–5 resulted in the Sibthorp Herbarium, a core element of the Oxford Herbaria, and the magnificent *Flora Graeca*, illustrated by artist Ferdinand Bauer, which is the 'jewel in the crown' of Oxford's botanical treasures. The spectacular quality of the *Flora*'s illustrations, its size (ten volumes with 966 plates) and its publication cost make the *Flora Graeca* one of the most extraordinary botanical volumes of all time. The voyages of Sibthorp and Bauer also bestowed a rich horticultural legacy through the introduction of popular garden plants to cultivation, including crocuses from Turkey and their many derived hybrids, and *Cyclamen persicum*, collected in Cyprus. The new planting of the Rock Garden reflects this important botanical, artistic and horticultural legacy.

Euphorbia rigida in bloom in the Rock Garden.

THE HERBACEOUS BORDER

This ever-popular border is a classic example
of the traditional English herbaceous border.
It is never the same year on year, as new
planting combinations are employed to
maximize its dramatic horticultural impact.
To ensure that its structural tapestry is
maintained throughout the summer, the taller
plants are supported by natural hazel and birch
staking, supplied by the Harcourt Arboretum.

Peonies (*Paeonia* cultivar).

The Herbaceous Border.

PLANTS THAT CHANGED THE WORLD

Since 2015 this area, which was previously used to cultivate vegetables in the style of an allotment, has been transformed into a showpiece collection, highlighting 'useful' plants that have changed the course of human civilizations across the globe.

In these borders there is a mixture of edible plants and those used for medicines, construction, fibres and dyes. They include very familiar food plants, such as wheat, potatoes, cabbages and sweetcorn, and a timeline records the history of their botanical immigration to the UK.

More 'plants that changed the world' can be found in the glasshouses, including coffee, tea, cocoa, rice, bananas and pineapple, as these everyday supermarket 'essentials' come from the tropical and subtropical parts of the world. Together these indoor and outdoor plantings illustrate the critical importance of plants to people's daily lives. Without plants there would not be life on earth.

Foxgloves (*Digitalis purpurea*) in the Plants that Changed the World Borders.

Tomatoes (*Solanum lycopersicum*, foreground) and a hardy banana
(*Musa basjoo*, background) in the Plants that Changed the World Borders.

THE GIN BORDER

This novel border displays plants that are used as botanicals to flavour alcohol, especially gin. Indeed, many of these plants are employed in the production of the Botanic Garden's own 'Oxford Physic Gin', which contains 25 botanicals that were grown in the original Physicke Garden in 1648.

The Merton Borders in midsummer.

THE MERTON BORDERS

The Garden worked in collaboration with
Professor James Hitchmough of the
Department of Landscape Architecture at
the University of Sheffield to develop this
'prairie planting', reminiscent of Hitchmough's
famous planting design for the Olympic Park
at Stratford created with Sheffield colleague
Professor Nigel Dunnett for the 2012 London
Olympics. The Merton Borders, so called
because their central path runs towards the
tower of Merton College Chapel, currently
occupy an area of 955 square metres, and are
an example of sustainable low-maintenance

Echinacea (*Echinacea* cultivar) in flower in
the Merton Borders.

The Merton Borders in late summer.

horticultural development, with the aim of having minimal impact on the environment in the long term.

The planting is inspired by natural drought-tolerant prairie plant communities to produce an ornamental yet sustainable display. They originate from three seasonally dry grassland communities: the North American prairies; the South African Drakensberg grasslands; and the Eurasian Steppes. Most of the plants were established through the direct sowing of seed. This has two benefits: firstly, it is more sustainable than planting thousands of specimens grown in peat-based composts and plastic containers; secondly, sowing from seed makes it possible to establish plants at much higher densities. This increases the diversity of the plantings and ensures a long succession of flowering through the season.

The dynamic style of planting is colourful from early summer to early autumn. Being drought-tolerant, it requires no irrigation or fertilizers. It is allowed to die back through autumn and into winter, when it provides a rich habitat for many seed-eating small birds and mammals.

THE WATER GARDEN

The Water Garden is situated around an
artificial pond in the lowest-lying part of the
Garden where it provides a damp, boggy
environment for marginal plants. It is managed
less intensively than other sections of the
Garden, which gives the planting a more
naturalistic feel. A mixture of exotic and
native species is grown here. The native bog
bean (*Menyanthes trifoliata*) can be seen in
the pond, while the large leaves of *Gunnera
manicata* from Brazil dominate the central
island. The majority of the plants are early
flowering, so this area is at its most colourful

in late spring, with the blossoming of extensive stands of *Iris sibirica*, *Darmera peltata* and the native marsh marigold (*Caltha palustris*). Further interest is provided by the bold foliage of a number of marginal plants, such as species of *Rheum*, *Rodgersia*, *Ligularia* and *Hosta*. The pond not only increases the diversity of plants that can be grown in the Garden, but also increases the diversity of its fauna: newts, frogs, dragonflies and damselflies all thrive, as well as nesting moorhens and coots.

Under the dogwood (*Cornus mas*) to the east side of the Water Garden is a bench that has become a place of pilgrimage for fans of Philip Pullman's trilogy *His Dark Materials*, for it is here that the central characters Lyra and Will meet between their respective worlds. The bed under the dogwood has been planted to reflect places Lyra visits in the books, most notably Lapland and Svalbard in *Northern Lights* (1995). Plants evoking these arctic regions and the colours of the aurora borealis include various grasses and species of Jacob's ladder (*Polemonium*), *Geranium* and foxglove (*Digitalis*).

THE
FUTURE

Oxford Botanic Garden has been a centre
of botanical research where people have
marvelled at the scientific wonder
of plants for centuries. As we look to
the future botanic gardens cannot be
complacent. The world is experiencing
unprecedented transformation in terms
of its climate and human population
growth, placing a burgeoning demand on
the food resources of the planet. Plants
provide all human food either directly or
indirectly and our future depends on the
sustainable use of plants. Botanic gardens
must promote this message through
education at all levels and help deliver
solutions to the problems associated with
global change through their scientific
research and conservation programmes.
In a frenetic world, botanic gardens are
also green oases where people can relax
and find spiritual and mental well-being.
Originally conceived as medicinal gardens,
botanic gardens can thus once again
become important places for
human healing.

TIMELINE

1621 Oxford Physicke Garden founded by Sir Henry Danvers, 1st Earl of Danby KG

1632 The Danby Gate completed

1642 Jacob Bobart the Elder made first keeper

1645 The yew, the Garden's oldest tree, is planted

1648 First published list of the Garden's plants

1669 Robert Morison appointed first Professor of Botany at Oxford

1679 Bobart the Younger made keeper

1728 William Sherard leaves a legacy to endow a professorial chair in botany

1733 Two conservatories designed by William Townesend constructed

1734 Johann Jacob Dillenius becomes the first Sherardian Professor of Botany

1736 Carl Linnaeus, 'The father of taxonomy', visits the Garden

1749 First pineapple grown

1750 Botanical artist Georg Dionysius Ehret employed as a gardener

1784 John Sibthorp appointed Sherardian Professor of Botany

1788 Ferdinand Bauer paints Greek flowers for *Flora Graeca*

1813 William Baxter appointed head gardener

1834 Charles Daubeny appointed Sherardian Professor and renames the garden Oxford Botanic Garden

1837 Baxter and Daubeny redesign the Garden

1851 Glasshouses built in their current location

1853 Amazonian water lily flowers for the first time

1880/4 Taxonomic Beds introduced; Department of Botany formed at the Garden

1880s First laboratory set up for the Botany Department

1893 Glasshouses rebuilt

1926 The Rock Garden is first constructed

1940s The Lower Garden annexed; first female gardeners employed

1951 Department of Botany relocated to the University Science Area, South Parks Road

1963 Harcourt Arboretum becomes part of the Botanic Garden

1971 Glasshouses rebuilt

1991 Friends of the Oxford Botanic Garden and Arboretum formed

2006 The Charlotte Building completed

2010 The Oxford Florilegium Society formed

2015 The Plants that Changed the World Beds created

2016 The Cheshire Cat appears in the new Literary Woodland

2018 The Herbarium Room opened

2021 400th anniversary of Oxford Botanic Garden